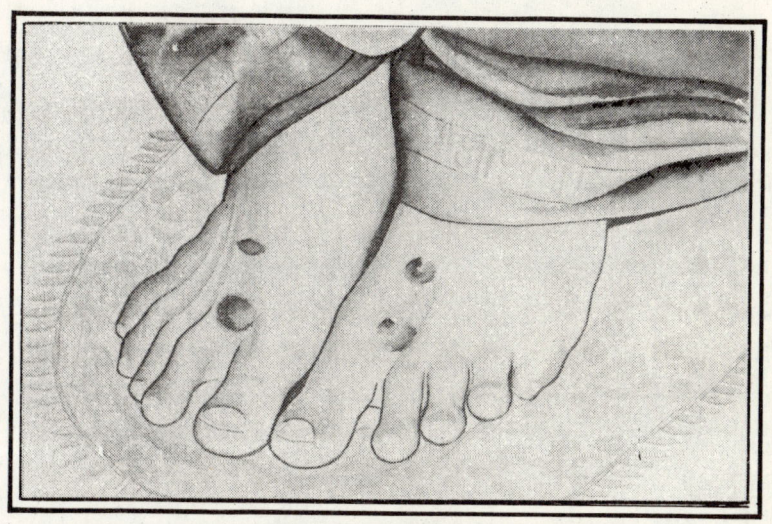

This offering is placed at
the Lotus Feet of
Bhagavan Sri Sathya Sai Baba
with love and devotion

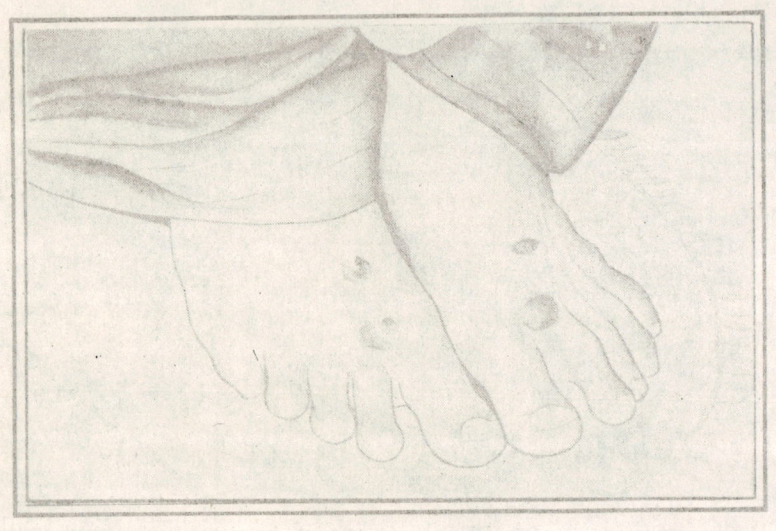

This offering is placed at
the Lotus Feet of
Bhagavan Sri Sathya Sai Baba
with love and devotion

Words of Truth

A second compilation of sayings by

Bhagavan Sri Sathya Sai Baba

in calligraphical script by
Andrew Shaw

A Sterling Paperback

STERLING PAPERBACKS
An imprint of
Sterling Publishers Private Limited

L-10, Green Park Extension,
New Delhi-110016

Words of Truth
More Sayings of Bhagavan
Sri Sathya Sai Baba

ISBN 81 207 1905 0

Reprint 1998

Published by Sterling Publishers Pvt. Ltd., New Delhi-110016.
Printed at Yougantar Prakashan (P) Ltd., Delhi-110064.
Cover design by Andrew Shaw

This book is dedicated
to the memory
of my brother-in-law
and friend – Pete –
whose life was
a shining example
of how to live
according to the
    Golden Rule :–
"Do unto others as
you would have others
do unto you."

This book is dedicated
to the memory
of my brother-in-law
and friend — Pete —
whose life was
a shining example
of how to live
according to the
Golden Rule :-
"Do unto others as
you would have others
do unto you."

To someone who does not know who Sai Baba is, I reply:

"Imagine if you had been alive at the time of Jesus and been able to be with Him: it is the same to be in the presence of Sai Baba. No – it is better. Because He is here NOW!"

Baba's love, guidance and wisdom have steered my pen to compile this second volume of His sayings. As I was completing the manuscript, I learned of the death of Dr. John Hislop, from whose book "My Baba and I" some of this text is taken. My grateful thanks to a wonderful soul, who was as close as any to Swami for so many years.

Other sources for material for this volume come from Baba's "Thought of the Day" board at Prasanthi, as well as quotes from Dr. Naresh Bhatia's beautiful book, "The Dreams and Realities Face to Face with God". Also I have chosen a selection from the calendar published by Prasanthi - which keeps me close to Swami on a daily basis.

My gratitude to all these sources, as the work continues to bring the Truth of Sathya Sai to an ever-widening audience.

🕉

Om Sai Ram !

Afterword

Today is the first anniversary of the death of my brother-in-law Pete, to whom this book is dedicated.

Just a few weeks ago, another great soul passed this mortal coil — Sir George Trevelyan. It seems appropriate that this Champion of Truth should be linked to this book, since Sai Baba has declared 1996 The Year of Truth. Let me complete this work with a quote from Coleridge, one of Sir George's favourite writers :-

"There is one mind,
One omnipresent mind, Omnific.
His most holy name is Love.
Truth of subliming import !"

2 March 1996   Andrew Shaw

Contents

Contents

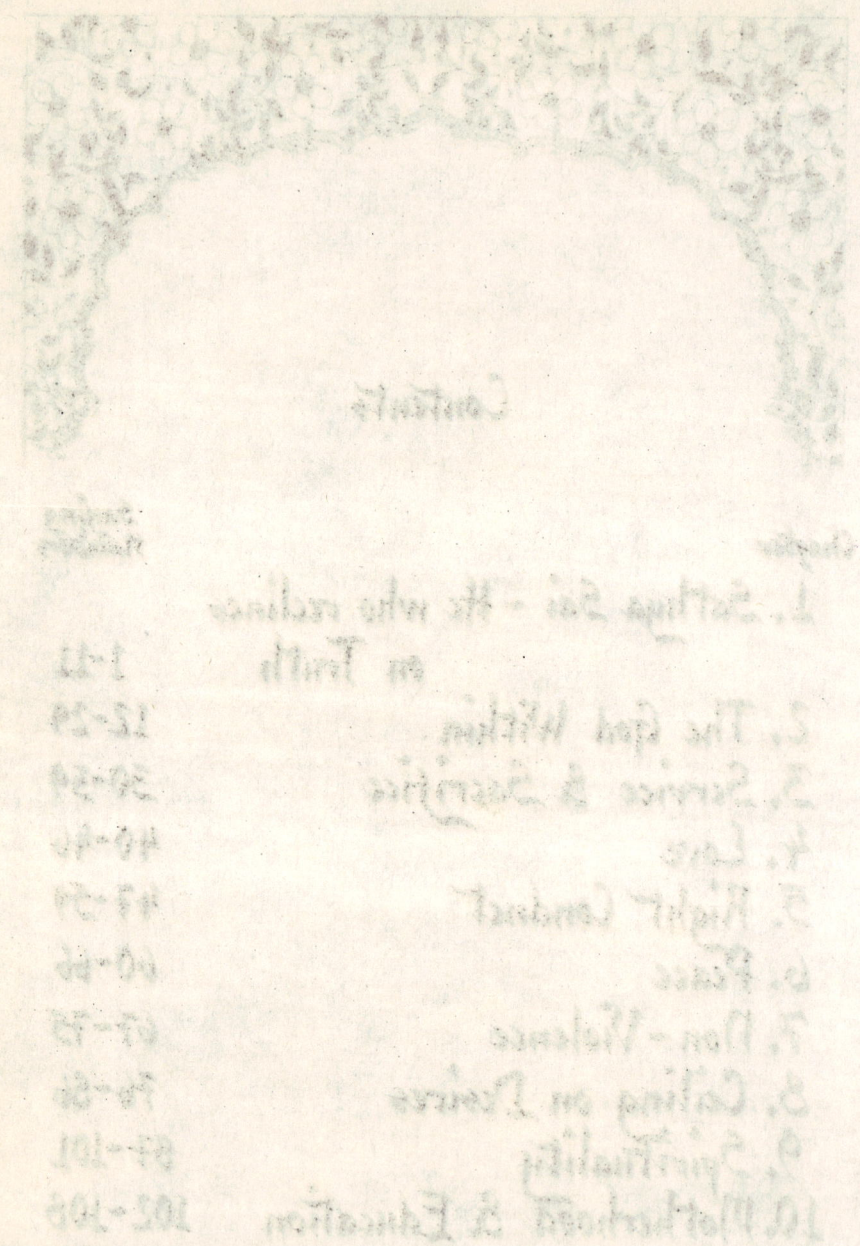

Chapter One

Sathya Sai

He who reclines on Truth

Sadhus prayed
and I have come.
When Dharma declines,
    I restore it
        and put down the forces
            which cause the decline,
by assuming a form —
    and I am born again and again
    in every crisis
        in order to protect the good,
            punish the wicked
                and restore Dharma.
That is why the present Avatar
    has come, invested with
        the totality of cosmic power
            to save Dharma
                from anti-Dharma.

This Sai has come
in order to achieve
the supreme task
of uniting as one family
the entire mankind,
through the bond of brotherhood;
of affirming and illumining
the Atmic Reality
of each being,
in order to reveal the Divine,
which is the basis on which
the entire Cosmos rests.

Before the beginning of things
only the Cosmic Consciousness existed,
and I am that
Cosmic Consciousness.
In the beginning there was nothing,
just an endless void,
but I was always there,
the Origin,
the true Beginning.
In a way there was no beginning,
however, as I always was,
always have been,
and always will be.

Let Me tell you one thing :
However you are,
                you are Mine.
I will not give you up.
Wherever you are,
                you are near Me ;
you cannot go
                beyond My Reach.

All forms of power
    are resident
        in this Sai palm.
My power is immeasurable;
my Truth is inexplicable,
        unfathomable.
I am announcing this about Me,
for the need has arisen.

You cannot see Me,
  but I am the Light
  you see by.
You cannot hear Me,
  but I am the Sound
  you hear by.
You cannot know Me,
  but I am the Truth
  by which you live.

You have not heard Me fully;
I say I am God;
I say also that you are God.
The difference is
that I know it
and you do not know it.

The story of the Lord's 'Leela'
is all Nectar;
it has no other component,
no other taste,
no other content.
Everyone can drink his fill,
from any part
of that Ocean of Nectar.
The same sweetness
exists everywhere,
in every particle.
There is nothing inferior
to mar the sweetness.

Baba showers this ash (Vibhuthi)
from His palm,
His forehead,
His feet
and His pictures.
For His devotees
this gift of ash
is the panacea
for all physical,
mental
and intellectual illness.
Baba is indeed
"Maheswara".

Love, respect, tolerance,
   mutual cooperation, forbearance –
      these must flow
         from the hearts of all
            towards all;
you are all limbs of one body –
      the Sai body.
Love is joy.
            Love is power.
      Love is light.
                  Love is God.
If at all you want
            to label Me,
      then call Me "Premswarup".
      Love is
            the keynote of harmony.

Work, worship and wisdom
　are the three stages
　　on the godward path.
Love leads to expansion;
　hatred leads to contraction.
　Love lives by
　　　giving and forgiving,
self lives by
　　　getting and forgetting.
Selfless love is
　the source of happiness,
truth, peace,
　　　sacrifice, endurance,
and all other
　　　higher values
　　　　of life.

"Willing" is superfluous for Me,
    for My Grace is ever-available
    to devotees who have
        steady faith and love.
Since I move among them
    talking and singing,
    even the intellectuals
are unable to grasp My Truth,
    My Power, Glory or
        My real task as Avatar.
I can solve any problem,
                however knotty.
I am beyond the reach
of the most intense inquiry
    and the most meticulous
                measurement.

Only those who have recognised
      My Love and experienced
that Love can assert that they
have glimpsed My reality, for The
      path of Love is the royal road
that leads mankind to Me.
I am all forms ascribed to the
Almighty : I am the Embodiment of
      Perfect Peace.   I am known by
all The Names through which
      the Almighty is addressed and
      adored by Man. I am the
Embodiment of Goodness ; I am
Being ~ Awareness, Bliss, Atma,
the One without a Second ;
      Truth, Goodness, Beauty.

Chapter Two

The God Within

You are three people:

The one you think you are –
　　　　　　　　body.

The one others think you are –
　　　　　　　　mind.

The one you really are –
　　　　　　　　divine.

God is the echo of the hills,
    the fruits of the leaves,
        the whisper of men,
    the babble of children
and the Aum that is wafted everywhere.
God is present at all places;
    but to recognise Him Saints have
had to prescribe a thousand methods.
    He is everyone,
        yet He evades discovery
            by all but a few,
                being all-powerful.
He is the giver of all gifts,
    the providence bestowing upon us all
                the wherewithal.
He remains all-encompassing.

Faith is the basis of every act.
  You do not run away from the barber
because he is armed with a sharp razor.
    You place faith in him
  and allow him to cut your hair,
quietly submitting to his idiosyncrasies.
      You give away costly clothes
  to the Dhobi, since you have
    the faith that he will return
        them washed and ironed.
  You have faith in the driver
    of your car and the engineer
        who built your house.
So too believe in the inner
  motivator, the Atma within,
        the voice of God.

Remember that with every step
  you are nearing God, and God, too,
when you take one step towards Him,
          takes ten towards you.
There is no stopping place
          in this pilgrimage;
it is one continuous journey,
  through day and night, through
valley and desert, through tears
  and smiles, through death and
birth, through tomb and womb.
  When the road ends, and the
    goal is gained, the pilgrim
    finds that he has travelled only
      from himself to himself,
that the way was long and lonesome,
  but the God that led him unto,
was all the while in him, around
him, with him and beside him.

Life is a pilgrimage, where man
  drags his feet along
        the rough and thorny road.
With the Name of God on his lips,
    he will have no thirst;
with the Form of God in his heart,
    he will feel no exhaustion.
The company of the holy
    will inspire him to travel
            in hope and faith.
The assurance that God is
                within call,
    that He is ever near,
      nor is He long in coming,
will lend strength to his limbs
        and courage to his eye.

Let the petty wishes for which
        you now approach God
            be realised or not,
    let the plans for promotion
and progress which you place
before God, be fulfilled or not;
        they are not so important after all.
The primary aim should be
        to become Masters of yourselves,
            to hold intimate and constant
    communion with the Divine that
                is in you
as well as in the Universe
            of which you are a part.
Welcome disappointments,
        for they toughen you
            and test your fortitude.

The foundation for real peace is,
   according to the Vedas,
     the quality of My Three.
My Three means
   amicability, compassion, kindness.
It can also be taken to mean
   "my three",
     that is to say,
my word, deed and
   thought shall be in accordance
   with thy word,
     thought and deed.
That is to say,
   we shall speak, think
     and act together,
without friction or faction, in the
atmosphere of love and understanding.
That is what is wanted in the
   world today, My Three.

The Grace of God
is not easily attainable.
The feeling of I-ness -
Ahamkara - which makes one say
"I am the doer"
should be plucked by the roots
from the heart.
Everyone, be he learned
or illiterate, should feel an
overwhelming urge to know God.
God has equal affection towards
all His children,
for to illumine
is the nature of light.

The awareness of the Atma
or the Divine in man
can neither be gifted to another,
nor be accepted from another -
it is all the time hidden
behind the veil of ignorance.
When the false image disappears,
the truth shines
in all its glory.
It is like the sun
behind the passing cloud.
Your duty is to draw away
this veil and let
the sun of awareness
shine forth and illumine
your thoughts, words and deeds.

Those who teach about Nature
                    and its laws,
matter and its properties,
    forces and their pulls,
        teach to bind,
            not to liberate.
It is a burden, not bliss.
    It provides a stone boat
        for you to cross the sea
            with waves of grief
    and crests of joy.
It cannot
    float you along;
        it is certain
            to sink.

What you need to cross the sea
      is the bark of bhakthi,
of assurance of Grace,
   of surrender to His will.
    Throw off all burdens,
      become light,
and you can trip across
with one step on one crest
   and another on the next.
God will take you through.
   You have no need
    to bother at all.
  For,
    when He does everything,
    who is concerned about what?

Faith
  is like
    our life-breath.
It is impossible
  to live
    even for a minute
      in this world
        without Faith.

If you feel
you are
a hundred per cent
dependent on God
He will look after you
and save you
from harm
and injury.

You sit in meditation for ten minutes
 after the evening Bhajan session;
  so far, so good.
But, let me ask,
 when you rise after the ten
  minutes and move about,
 do you see everyone in a
      clearer light
 as endowed with Divinity?
   If not, meditation
     is a waste of time.
Do you love more,
  do you talk less,
do you serve others more earnestly?
  These are the signs
    of success in meditation.

Your progress must be authenticated
        by your character
                and behaviour.
Meditation must transmute
    your attitude towards beings
    and things, else it is a hoax.
Even a boulder will,
    through the action of sun and rain,
            heat and cold,
        disintegrate into mud
                and become food
                    for a tree.
Even the hardest heart
            can be softened
    so that the Divine
            can sprout therein.

God
gave you
the time, space,
cause, material, idea,
skill, chance
and fortune.
Why should you feel
as if
you are the doer?

Without Sleep,
  man, as well as
    other beings,
      cannot live.
Of all the joys
  that the world provides,
    Sleep is
      the most rewarding.

He is in you, and it is God
that has prompted you to project
Him into the outer world,
as this idol or that image,
to listen to your outpouring
and give you peace.
Without the inspiration, solace and
joy that He confers from within,
you will be raving mad,
as one who has lost his moorings
and is tossed about,
rudderless on a stormy sea.
Hold on to Him in the heart,
hear Him whisper
in the silent words
of counsel and consolation.

Hold converse with Him,
          guide your footsteps
                    as He directs,
and you reach the goal,
          safe and soon.
The picture before which you sit,
     the flowers which you place on it,
          the hymns you recite,
                    the vows
     you impose on yourselves,
          the vigils you go through —
these are activities
                    that cleanse,
     that remove obstacles
in the way of your getting aware
     of the God within.

Practise Silence:
for the Voice of God
can be heard
in the region
of your heart
only when the tongue
is stilled and
storm is stilled,
and the waves are calm.

When the road ends,
and the goal is gained,
the pilgrim finds
that he has travelled
only from himself
to himself.

Chapter Three

Service
&
Sacrifice

You must render service
out of spontaneous urge
from within,
with a heart
filled
with love.

To remove the evils of egoism
service is the most
efficient instrument.
Service will also impress on the
person doing service
the unity of all mankind.
He who dedicates his time, skill
and strength will never meet with
defect, distress or disappointment,
for service is its own reward.
His word will be ever sweet
and soft and his gestures
ever revered and humble.
He will have no foe,
no fatigue and no fear.

Faith in God
is the secure foundation
on which hope has to be built.
The faith has to be
stable and strong.
The feeling that God
will come to our rescue
has to be vivid and vital,
motivating and activating
all that we do or speak or think.
Service rendered to others
in this spirit
will be a great
source of joy to us
as well as to the recipient.

Service in all its forms,
    all the world over,
is primarily
            spiritual discipline –
mental clean-up!
Without the inspiration
    given by that attitude,
        the urge is bound to ebb
                and grow dry, or
it may meander
            into pride and pomp.
Just think for a moment :
    Are you
            serving God?
                    Or
    is God serving you? . . .

When you offer milk to
                a hungry child,
or a blanket to a
shivering brother on the pavement,
   you are but placing a gift of God
        into the hands of
           another gift of God !
You are reposing the gift of God
     in a repository
       of the Divine Principle !
God serves ; He allows you to claim
        that you have served !
Without His Will, no single blade
of grass can quiver in the breeze.
        Fill every moment with gratitude to
the Giver and Recipient of all gifts.

Service
should not be
exhibitionistic;
you must seek
no reward,
not even gratitude
or thanks
from the recipients.

The fulfilment
of human life
consists
in the service
that man renders,
without any thought
of return,
in an attitude
of selflessness.

The age span 16-30 is crucial,
for that is the period
when life adds sweetness to itself,
when talents, skills and
attitudes are accumulated,
sublimated and sanctified.
If the tonic of unselfish service
is administered to the mind
during this period,
life's mission is fulfilled –
for the process of
sublimation and
sanctification
will be hastened
by this tonic.

Do not serve for the sake
   of reward, attracting attention,
     or earning gratitude,
 or from a sense of pride
at your own superiority in skill,
   wealth, status or authority.
            Serve because
 you are urged by Love.
   When you succeed,
ascribe the success to the Grace
of God who urged you on, as Love
within you. When you fail,
      ascribe the failure to your
 own inadequacy, insincerity,
              or ignorance.

Small minds
  select
    narrow roads;
expand
  your mental vision
    and take to
      the broad road
of helpfulness,
  compassion
    and service.

One who has
the true spirit
of sacrifice
gives to others
without any hesitation
or reservation,
smilingly and gladly,
even his dearest
and highest possession.

The body
will shine
if the character
is fine ;
service of man
and
worship of God
will preserve
its charm.

Chapter Four

Love

The Lord
 will be watching
  with a
   thousand eyes
the least activity of man
 to discover
  any slight trace
   of selfless love
    sweetening it.

Friendship
is the expression
of unshakeable Love —
Love that is noble,
pure,
free from desire
or egoism.

Love as thought is Truth;
Love as action is Righteousness;
Love as feeling is Peace;
Love as understanding is
        Non-Violence.

See with the eyes of Love,
Hear with the ears of Love,
Work with the hands of Love,
Think of Love,
Feel Love in every nerve.

Life is a song, sing it;
Life is a game, play it;
Life is a challenge, meet it;
Life is a dream, realize it;
Life is a sacrifice, offer it;
Life is Love, enjoy it.

Have no thorn of hate in your mind,
   develop love towards everyone.
Desire is a storm,
                  greed is a whirlpool,
   pride is a precipice,
      attachment is an avalanche,
            egoism is a volcano.
Keep these things away so that
   when you recite the name of God
            or do meditation,
they do not disturb the equanimity.
   Let love be enthroned
               in your heart.
Then there will be sunshine and
         cool breezes and
   gurgling waters
                  of contentment
feeding the roots of faith.

Learn this lesson
    of light and love;
    move out,
        clasp, spread,
            expand,
    give up limits
        of mine and thine,
            his and theirs,
                caste and creed,
in one limitless flow of love.

Chapter Five

Right Conduct

Egoism will be destroyed,
  if you constantly tell yourself
      it is He, not I.
He is the force, I am
          but the instrument.
Keep His name always on the tongue
  and contemplate His glory,
whenever you see or hear anything
        beautiful or grand.
See in everyone the Lord Himself
        moving in that form.
Do not talk evil of others;
see only good in them and
      welcome every chance
      to help others
      and to encourage others
      along the spiritual path.

The synthesis
of pure, calming food
is breathing pure air,
listening to good sounds,
looking at good sights,
and touching pure objects.

If the mind of man
is not reformed
and purified
then all the plans
to reform the world
will be futile.

Condemn the wrong
and
  extol the right
as soon as you notice
  either in your children;
that will settle them
  on the straight path.

Make the fullest
of your talents
and march
as long as you can,
and pitch the Tent
nearer the goal
when darkness falls.

Use the eyes to watch
          wholesome things,
the feet to proceed
          to the home of God,
the hands to serve the
    embodiments of God
moving around you as men,
          and the tongue to soothe
the pain, praise virtue and
                glorify God.
Do not use your eye
    to vulgarise your brain,
or your feet to stand in queue
    for deleterious movie shows.

Many of you have problems
        of health and
mental worry
        of some sort or other.
They are mere baits by which
        you have been brought here,
so that you may contact
the Grace and strengthen
        your faith in the Divine.
                Problems and worries
are really to be welcomed
        as they teach you
the lesson of
humility and reverence.

Do not get swelled up
when people praise you
and
do not feel dejected
when people blame you.

Your thoughts,
words and deeds
will shape others,
and theirs
will shape you.

It is best
to live with honour
for just a day
than with dishonour
for many decades:
better a short-lived
celestial swan
than
a century-lived crow.

We should realize
   that man
      has not only a mind
         which conceives thoughts,
but also a heart
      which can put them
         into practice.

Children must grow up
  in an atmosphere
    of reverence,
      devotion,
    mutual service
    and cooperation.
They must be taught respect
  for parents, teachers
    and elders.
Children must grow
  in the awareness
    of the brotherhood of man
    and fatherhood of God.

Make your heart soft,
        then success is quick
in Sadhana (spiritual practice).
Talk softly, talk sweetly,
        talk only of God –
that is the process
        of softening the subsoil.
Develop compassion, sympathy;
        engage in service,
        understand the agony
of poverty and disease,
        distress and despair;
share both tears and cheers with others.
That is the way
        to soften the heart
and help Sadhana to succeed.

Chapter Six

Peace

Hatred sprouts;
  Envy raises its hood.
Love sprouts;
  Peace descends like dew.

The peace
that pervades
the heart
can never be shaken
for any reason;
only peace
of this kind
is worthy
of
the name.

World peace
  and individual peace
    can be accomplished
      simultaneously.
When the hand
  takes food to the mouth
    where it is chewed
      and swallowed,
the nourishment spreads
  to every part of the body.

By peace,
western countries mean
the interval
between two wars.
That is no peace !
When man thinks,
speaks and does good —
peace will ensue.

Man is now able
to soar into outer space
and reach up
to the moon;
but he is not moral enough
to live at peace
with his neighbour.

When the Name is pronounced
by the tongue,
and the Image is adored
by the mind,
these should not degenerate
into mechanical routine;
the Meaning of the Name
and the content of the Form must,
at the same time,
inspire and illumine the consciousness.
Escape the routine;
involve yourselves in
the attitude of worship,
deeply and sincerely.
That is the way to earn
peace and contentment,
for which all human activity
ought to be
dedicated and directed.

Detachment, Faith and Love —
these are the pillars
on which Peace rests.
Of these, Faith is crucial.
For, without it, Sadhana
(spiritual practice) is an empty rite.
Detachment alone can make
Sadhana effective and Love
leads quickly to God.
Faith feeds the agony of
separation from God;
Detachment canalises it along
the path of God; Love lights
the way. God will grant you
what you need and deserve;
there is no need to ask,
no reason to grumble. Be content,
be grateful whatever happens.
Nothing can happen against His will.

Chapter Seven

Non ~ Violence

Base your action on knowledge,
  the knowledge that all is One.
Let the action be suffused
    with bhakti; that is to say,
        humility, love,
      mercy and non-violence.
Let bhakti be filled with knowledge,
  otherwise it will be as light
as a balloon which drifts
    along any current of air,
          or gust of wind.
Mere knowledge will make
  the heart dry; bhakti makes it
soft with sympathy, and karma
gives the hands something to do,
    something which will sanctify
        every one of the minutes
that have fallen to your lot to live.

Speak soft and sweet;
sympathise with suffering
and loss
and ignorance:
try your best
to apply the salve
of soothing words
and timely succour.

There should not be
any trace of dislike
or distrust
    on the score of
nationality,
language, caste,
economic status,
scholarship,
age or sex.

Those who have gone through
pain and suffering
can understand
and sympathise
with those
who are in pain
and those who suffer.

While Science has overcome
the barriers of time,
distance and nationality,
it has done little
to promote
better understanding
between man and man,
nation and nation.

Renunciation
is the power
of battling against
evil forces
and holding the mind
in check.

Do not use
poisonous words
against anyone,
for words wound
more fatally
than even arrows.

Let the different faiths exist,
let them flourish,
    and let the glory of God
    be sung
in all the languages
    and
in a variety of tunes.

Cleanse your emotions,
   passions, impulses,
      attitudes and reactions.
That is the essence of
   spiritual discipline as laid down
      in all faiths.
         Examine your mind,
            your thoughts,
do not seek the fault-ridden person.
      Seek only purity.
Speak ill of none.
      Do not humiliate anyone.
Respect each
   for the good in him.

Chapter Eight

Ceiling on Desires

Do not get attached
to worldly things
and pursuits.
Be in the world,
but do not let the world
be in you.

Man has been enslaved by money.
  He lives a superficial, hollow life.
This is indeed a great pity.
Man should seek to possess
  only as much money as is most
      essential for his living.
The quantity of riches one must earn
can be compared to shoes one wears:
  if too small they cause pain;
    if too big they are a hindrance
to physical and mental comfort.
      When we have more
  it breeds pride, sloth
      and contempt for others.

In pursuit of money
   man descends to
      the level of the beast.
Money is of the nature
      of manure :
piled up in one place, it pollutes
   the air ; spread it wide,
scatter it over fields,
   it rewards you with
      a bumper harvest. So too,
when money is spent in all the
four quarters for promoting good
works, it yields contentment
   and happiness in plenty.

In western countries now, God is denied,
and man is relying on himself.
He exaggerates his own intelligence
and sense of adventure and prides
   himself on the advance he has made
       through science and technology.
But, intelligence without equanimity
   is filling mental hospitals.
Peace is fleeing from the hearts
           of men and women;
   social harmony is becoming
   a distant dream,
international concord is a mirage
           pursued by a few.
Man travels to the moon,
   but does not explore his own
   inner levels of consciousness,
and understanding them,
cleanse them and control them.

Sense control will guard you against
a host of evils. Do not believe that
because you are equipped with the
senses, nothing harmful can happen
through their free exercise.
You may have your car registered
in your own name and be driving
it yourself, but if you do not apply
the brakes in time, accidents are
bound to be your lot. Your body
can be compared to a car: your eyes
are like lights; your stomach the
petrol tank; your mouth the horn;
your mind the steering wheel.
Dharma, Artha, Karma, Moksha
the wheels; the air within the
tyres is faith; and
intelligence the switch.

Examine this question, for example:
Is man enslaved
    by external objects
        and the attraction
            they exercise over him?
Or is it some inner impulse
    that urges him forward
        to shackle himself to sorrow?
            I shall give an example ~
There are professional
                monkey~catchers
    in the villages
who employ a crude device
                for the purpose.
They place in the orchards
    or gardens infested
            by the marauders

a number of narrow-necked
earthen pots, with a handful
of peanuts inside each.
    The monkey approaches the pot,
knows that it has delicious nuts
inside, puts its long hand in
and collects the nuts in its fist.
    Now it finds it cannot
            take its arm out;
the neck is too narrow
for the nut-full fist!
    So it sits,
        helpless and forlorn,
            and is easily caught
and transported.
It thinks that there is
        someone inside

who is holding back its arm,
    when it tries to take it out !
        If only it had loosened
                the grip
and got rid of the attachment
                    to the nuts,
            it could have escaped !
So, too, you are the victims
of desire and the attachments
    that the desire entails.
You are bound by the shackles
    you have fastened around you !
        Liberation, too, is in your hands.
            Contemplate the unchanging
Glory of God ; then desire for the
transient baubles of the earth will
fade and you can be free.

Man must withstand
both praise and blame,
success and failure, pleasure and pain.
He must strive to be steadfast
and unmoved.
Once you collect desires,
you become their slave;
you will find no end to them.
When they are attained,
others assail you and
still leave you discontented.
Be aware of your innate divinity
and show these recurring desires
their due place.
The Soul in you is unaffected
by desire or defeat
or victory;
they are passing clouds.

Man seeks to change
the foods
available in nature
to suit his tastes,
thereby putting an end
to the very essence
of life
contained in them.

You must be as a lotus,
    unfolding its petals
        when the sun
            rises in the sky,
unaffected by the slush
    where it is born
        or even the water
            which sustains it !

Do not cultivate
    too much attachment
        to things of the world,
which appeal to
            carnal desires
            and sensual thirsts.
A moment comes
    when you have to depart
        empty-handed,
leaving all that you have
        laboriously collected
and proudly
            called your own.

God is the vastest among the vast,
 minutest among the minute,
  yet God has no ego.
   How then can man, who has
no claim to even the tiniest glory,
 parade himself as great?
It is really a ridiculous pose.
    The egoist ignores
the source which can bring
    respect to him.
He loses the chance
     of developing
his skills and talents
     on the right lines.

The morning shadow
            moves in front of you.
    However fast you run,
            you cannot catch it,
            on plain or mountain.
Or, the shadow may pursue you
and you cannot escape from it.
This is the nature of desire.
        You may pursue it
            or it may pursue you ~
but you cannot overcome it
                    or catch it.
Desire is an insubstantial shadow.
    But turn desire inward,
            towards spiritual treasure,
        then it yields
                substantial results.

Chapter Nine

Spirituality

When we sit down
for a meal,
we feel light
and effortless.
When we are done,
we should rise
with the same feeling
of lightness
and effortlessness.

The food we consume
should be tasty,
sustaining
and pleasant.
It should not be
too hot or too salty;
there must be
a balance and
an equilibrium
maintained.

There may be differences
among men –
   in physical strength,
   financial status,
      intellectual acumen –
but all are equal
   in the eyes of God.

Humans are born
with a helpless
lamenting cry;
they should die
with the smile
of happy joy.

The Body is like a flashlight,
the Eye is like the bulb,
   the Mind is the battery cell,
      the Intelligence is the switch;
only when the four
   work together
      do you get the light.

Light spreads;
it mingles with the light
from other sources
of light;
it has no boundaries,
no prejudices,
no favourites.

The grace of God
is like
insurance.
It will help you
in your time of need
without any limit.

Every living being
in this world
is knowingly
or unknowingly
on
a spiritual pilgrimage.

Man
will realize
his mission
on earth
when he knows himself
as Divine
and reveres others
as Divine.

The lights have
to be switched on
in the heart of man,
rather than
in the house where
the image of the Lord
is installed
and worshipped.

When a tree first shoots forth
 from the seed, it comes up with
a stem and two incipient leaves!
But later, when it grows,
        the trunk is one,
    and the branches are many!
Each branch may be thick enough
        to be called a trunk,
 but one should not forget
      that the roots send food
as sap through one single trunk.
       God, the same God,
feeds the spiritual hunger of
  all nations and all faiths,
through the common sustenance
       of truth, virtue,
   humility and sacrifice.

You may say that progress
        is possible only
                through My Grace,
but though My Heart
                is soft as butter,
it melts only when there is
some warmth in your prayer.
Unless you make some
            disciplined effort,
    some Sadhana,
Grace cannot descend on you.
The yearning, the agony of
            unfulfilled aim —
that is the warmth
        that melts My Heart.
That is the anguish
        that wins Grace.

You have to cultivate
    four types of strength.
Strength of body,
                intellect,
            discrimination
            and conduct.
Then you become unshakeable;
        you are
            on the path
    of spiritual victory.

The whole world is
  One Single Tree;
the different countries
      are its branches;
 its root is God;
human beings
      are the flowers;
 happiness is the fruit;
self-realization is
      the sweet juice therein.

God is Omnipotent –
    All – Powerful.

God is Omnipresent –
    Present Everywhere.

God is Omniscient –
    All – Knowing.

Chapter Ten

Motherhood
&
Education

The first thing which is
of importance to man and
to human nature
is his own behaviour.
After that comes discipline:
after that comes duty:
lastly - and finally -
comes devotion.
Discipline, Duty, Devotion
and Behaviour - these four
things together constitute
human nature.
This human nature is like
a mansion which rests
on these four pillars.

The child has its tongue
 and the mother has hers.
The mother keeps the child on her lap
 and pronounces the words
so that the child may learn to speak.
 However busy the mother's tongue
may be, the child has to speak
 through its own tongue.
The mother cannot speak for the child
 and save herself all the bother!
The Guru, too, is like that.
 He can only repeat, remind,
instruct, persuade, plead;
 the activity,
 the disciple must himself initiate.
He must jump over the stile himself.
 No one can hoist
 him over it!

Motherhood is
    the most precious gift of God.
Mothers are
        the makers of a nation's
    fortune or misfortune,
    for they shape the sinews of its soul.
            Those sinews
    are toughened by two lessons
        they should teach:
            fear of sin,
    and fondness for virtue.
        Both these
        are based on
            faith in God
                being
    the inner motivator
                of all.

If you want to know
      how advanced a nation is,
         study the mothers:
are they Free from
                  fear and anxiety,
      are they full of Love
                     towards all,
are they trained in fortitude and virtue?
If you like to imbibe
         the glory of a culture,
watch the mothers,
   rocking the cradles, feeding,
         fostering, teaching
and Fondling the babies.
As the mother, so the progress
of the nation; as the mother,
   so the sweetness of the culture.

Base all educational efforts
on building up
the character
of the students,
and then
you can confidently
think of raising on it
the superstructure
of curricula.

Either the Government
must have the capacity
to educate and
reform the people,
or the people
must have the capacity
to educate
the Government.

Modern education develops
the intellect and imparts skill,
but does not promote
good qualities in any way.
Of what value is
the acquisition of all
the knowledge in the world,
if there is no character?
Knowledge has multiplied
and with it desires have grown;
the result is that one is a 'hero'
in words, but a 'zero' in actions.
What is the use of acquiring
intelligence and skills,
if even a small fraction
of what is learnt
is not put into practice?

Teachers
are reservoirs
from which,
through the process
of education,
students draw
the water of life.

Glossary

Ahamkara	ego, pride
Artha	wealth to be earned through righteousness
Atma	the one infinite consciousness
Aum	primordial sound
Avatar	an incarnation of God
Bhakthi	devotion, love of God
Dharma	righteousness
Dhobi	washerman
Guru	"Dispeller of Darkness"
Karma	action and its reaction
Maheswara	great Lord
Moksha	liberation from the bondage of birth & death
Premswarup	embodiment of love
Sadhana	spiritual discipline
Sadhu	a good man — detached, wise, devoted, virtuous